World Language

Majid Khodabandeh
2021

Copyright © 2021 Magic Mason

All rights reserved. No part of this publication may be reproduced, distributed, or transmitted in any form or by any means, including photocopying, recording, or other electronic or mechanical methods, without the prior written permission of the publisher, except in the case of brief quotations embodied in critical reviews and certain other noncommercial uses permitted by copyright law. For permission requests, write to the publisher, addressed "Attention: Book Rights and Permission," at the address below.

Published in the United States of America

ISBN 978-1-955243-55-1 (SC)

Magic Mason
313 East Main St.
Mason OH 45040
www.mostimportantbooksforyourlife.com

Order Information and Rights Permission:

Quantity sales. Special discounts might be available on quantity purchases by corporations, associations, and others. For details, contact the publisher at the address above.

For Book Rights Adaptation and other Rights Permission. Call us at toll-free 1-888-945-8513 or send us an email at admin@stellarliterary.com.

Contents

Introduction: 1

Alphabet: 3

Numbers: 4

New Year: 10

Week Days: 11

English: 13

Fish and Chips with Mushy Peas 21

American Blueberry Pie: 24

Spanish: 27

Chicken Tortilla Soup 33

French: 35

Beef Barley Soup 42

Italian: 44

Four-Cheese Lasagna 51

Chinese: 53

Beef and Vegetable Stir-Fry 59

German: 61

Roasted Cheese Bagel Bites 67

Farsi: 69

White Rice 76

Japanese: 78

Arabic: **85**

Russian: **92**

Greek: **99**

Hindi: **106**

Southwest Black Bean Burgers 113

Brazilian (Portuguese): **115**

Mushroom and Epazote Tacos 122

Turkish: **124**

Ayran with Mint or Yogurt drink 130

References: **132**

Introduction:

My name is Majid Khodabandeh, U.S. Citizen, I was born in Tehran / Iran, and I have traveled all over the world, and have lived in Cincinnati, Ohio, and Northern Kentucky for the last 18 years. After many years of learning different languages and knowing that the language you speak it is not your native tongue, there are always consequences that you are not 100% native on those cultures. I feel that humans have a weakness and that they cannot speak the language perfectly, especially at the beginning of arrival to that country. I created this language book for the next generation, and it is a mix of 18 languages with basic words that are easy to memorize for all children to early adulthood, and this will add more vocabulary to the children's education. I recommend this book for every person. It is a very good reference book and teaches different cultures of language, and it will bring the world together so that human beings in the next generation will be able to speak in one language all over the world.

I start in the name of God who is still missing and which no one sees or has found him, and I will ask who is really GOD? We must try to know ourselves and know God with technology and good knowledge of surrounding, to bring God closer with the imagination of having a perfect world. I have to say life is short and we must make the best of that for our time on earth. To understand each other, we must believe in ourselves to communicate and understand the needs and live peacefully in the world.

I must say God bless you all, with kindest regards Majid Khodabandeh. I will present this book to all human beings, make best for all of you and your family, community and country and make a giving of freedom bell rings, and protect the freedom of writing and what we are saying with the right words.

This book is World Language which will be used all over the world.

Teachers and students, together in classrooms must read and memorize all of these words with repetition from kindergarten to 12th grade, and this book will be the same all the way to high school. A school must have disciplinary action and spend everyday at least for one hour to read and memorize part of this book.

This book will improve communication and open borders to other countries. Also, I encourage mixing race and communication, which will improve humanity.

This book also provides a new culture and custom to follow with good humanity values.

Alphabet:

Aa - Bb - Cc - Dd - Ee - Ff - Gg - Hh - Ii - Jj - Kk - Ll - Mm - Nn - Oo - Pp – Qq - Rr – Ss - Tt - Uu - Vv - Ww – Xx - Yy - Zz

Numbers:

1 – ONE
2 – TWO
3 – CEH
4 – FOUR
5 – FIVE
6 – SIX
7 – SEVEN
8 – EIGHT
9 – NOH
10 – TEN
11 – ELLEVEN
12 – TWELFE
13 – CEHTEN
14 – FOURTEN
15 – FIFTEN
16 – SIXTEN
17 – SEVENTEN
18 – EIGHTTEN
19 – NOHTEN
20 – BIST
21 – BISTONE
22 – BISTTOW
23 – BISCEH
24 – BISFOUR

Numbers

25 – BISFIVE
26 – BISSIX
27 – BISSEVEN
28 – BISEIGHT
29 – BISNOH
30 – CEHI
31 – CEHIONE
32 – CEHITOW
33 – CEHICEH
34 – CEHIFOUR
35 – CEHIFIVE
36 – CEHISIX
37 – CEHISEVEN
38 – CEHIEIGHT
39 – CEHINOH
40 – FORTY
41 – FORTHYONE
42 – FORTHYTWO
43 – FORTHYCEH
44 – FORTHYFOUR
45 – FOURTHYFIVE
46 – FOURTHYSIX
47 – FOURTHYSEVEN
48 – FOURTHYEIGHT
49 – FOURTHYNOH
50 – FIFTY
51 – FIFTYONE

Numbers

52 – FIFTYTWO
53 – FIFTYCEH
54 – FIFTYFOUR
55 – FIFTYFIVE
56 – FIFTYSIX
57 – FIFTYSEVEN
58 – FIFTYEIGHT
59 – FIFTYNOH
60 – SIXTY
61 – FIFTYONE
62 – SIXTYTWO
63 – SIXTYCEH
64 – SIXTYFOUR
65 – SIXTYFIVE
66 – SIXTYSIX
67 – SIXTYSEVEN
68 – SIXTYEIGHT
69 – SIXTYNOH
70 – SEVENTY
71 – SEVENTYONE
72 – SEVENTYTWO
73 – SEVENTYCEH
74 – SEVENTYFOUR
75 – SEVENTYFIVE
76 – SEVENTYSIX
77 – SEVENTYSEVEN
78 – SEVENTYEIGHT
79 – SEVENTYNOH

Numbers

80 – EIGHTY
81 – EIGHTYONE
82 – EIGHTYTWO
83 – EIGHTYCEH
84 – EIGHTYFOUR
85 – EIGHTYFIX
86 – EIGHTYSIX
87 – EIGHTYSEVEN
88 – EIGHTYEIGHT
89 – EIGHTYNOH
90 – NOHTY
91 – NOHTYONE
92 – NOHTYTWO
93 – NOHTYCEH
94 – NOHTYFOUR
95 – NOHTYFIVE
96 – NOHTYSIX
97 – NOHTYSEVEN
98 – NOHTYEIGHT
99 – NOHTYNOH
100 – SADD
101 – SADDONE
102 – SADDTWO
103 – SADDCEH
104 – SADDFOUR
105 – SADDFIVE
106 – SADDSIX
107 – SADDSEVEN

108 – SADDEIGHT
109 – SADDNOH
110 – SADDTEN
111 – SADDELEVEN
112 – SADDTWELF
113 – SADDCEHTEN
114 – SADDFOUR
115 – SADDFIVE
116 – SADDSIX
117 – SADDSEVEN
118 – SADDEIGHT
119 – SADDNOH
120 – SADDBIST
130 – SADDCEHI
140 – SADDFORTY
150 – SADDFIFTY
160 – SADDSIXTY
170 – SADDSEVENTY
180 – SADDEIGHTY
190 – SADDNOHTY
200 – TWOSADD
300 – CEHSADD
400 – FOURADD
500 – FIVEADD
600 – SIXADD
700 – SEVENADD
800 – EIGHTADD
900 – NOHADD

Numbers

1,000 – HEZAR
10,000 – TENHEZAR
100,000 – SADDHEZAR
1,000,000 – E' MILYON
1,000,000,000 – E' BILYON
1,000,000,000,000 – E' TERLYON

New Year:

The months will start with the first of the season of spring, which is called: 1st season. The 21st day of the old calendar will be the 1st of the months in the new calendar. Summer will be called: 2nd season, Fall will be called: 3rd season, and Winter will be called: 4th season.

New Year's will be filled with happiness, celebration, a big party and fireworks. After New Year's Day, I encourage you to visit all family and friends and neighbors during the 15 days after the new year.

New name		**Old name**		
1st months:	Earth	March	21st	1st season, spring
2nd months:	Tree	April		
3rd months:	Human	May		
4th months:	Fish	June		2nd season, summer
5th months:	Beef	July		
6th months:	Bread	August		
7th months:	Peace	September		3rd season, fall
8th months:	Clean	October		
9th months:	Save	November		
10th months:	Happy	December		4th season, winter
11th months:	Rain	January		
12th months:	Snow	February		

Week Days:

New days name   old name

1st day   Monday
2nd day   Tuesday
3rd day   Wednesday
4th day   Thursday   off day
5th day   Friday
6th day   Saturday
7th day   Sunday   off day

Three days off, is when employees have one day of the week where it will be the employees' choice day off. Full-time work will be 32 hours of work and everybody will have three days off. The minimum wage is $12.00 in 16 years after the millennium, and every 5 years, it will add $1.00 more. Minimum wages are based on the American economy until the entire world balances the economy. Eventually, everybody will use the same currency and it will be a global world economy. Global agriculture will be built, and there will be no more hunger and everybody will have work and transportation, shelter, and food on the table with the right partner or wife or husband; which must be easy access to everyone. I will encourage the partner to not have too many kids and a recommendation of a maximum of 2 kids.

It is better in the new world where we go with technology and every kid must have their own computer and to stay home and do the homework at home as the best option. Study will be from elementary to high school, all online. There is no more spending to build a school or university building; people don't have to pay school taxes and can improve the family economic status. Students will receive the homework online and they don't need to wake up early and ride the bus on cold or hot days.

Freedom of time is most important and there will be no more pressure for teachers or students to be in the classroom during early times of the day. There will not be a dress code or traffic to go to school. It will also cut out the violence in school and the stress and will save a lot of money.

The most important things are for learning world language. We must know a little English language to start this world language, which most kids in the world know basic English so far and the role of English. This book will cover simplified English grammar and spelling found in most conversations and written sentences. We can complete the sentences with this book vocabulary, but we must use all of the words in this book, and we must mix the languages with variations of vocabulary. I wrote 150 words or sentences for 13 languages, which all of the kids must learn these words during their 12 years of school. It must be mandatory in schools or home schooling, by parents. Study of this book for 12 years with the right pronunciation of each language is the key for success.

English:

English

English

1. Where is she?
2. She's outside.
3. She's eating.
4. I walk to school every day
5. I run to school every day.
6. I skip to school every day.
7. I'm going to school every day.
8. The women were bitten by the dog.
9. Which boy is in your class?
10. I didn't see Judy at the party.
11. There's a good restaurant down the street.
12. There's a drug store in the next block.
13. There are some new students in the class.
14. She may not have been there.
15. She had to finish a paper.
16. John was not in class when it began.
17. He might not have been on time.
18. He overslept this morning.

English

19. I got up late, so I didn't go to the store for bread.
20. I'm going to buy a coat and hat tonight.
21. If we receive some money, we will go to New York City.
22. If we go to New York City, we will go by plane.
23. He teaches the class every day.
24. Then he taught the class yesterday.
25. No, he didn't teach it yesterday
26. Why not? She makes a cake every weekend.
27. Roya has a date every weekend.

28. Majid makes a long-distance phone call every Sunday with his family.
29. Could you tell me the time?
30. Could you speak English?
31. Before you came?
32. Could you go tomorrow?
33. Could he come late?
34. Possibily
35. Could she cook before she was married?
36. Could you lend me a dime?
37. I write to my parents.
38. I will pay my bills by Monday.
39. I was going to study world language.
40. The girl who is coming is my sister.
41. I was in Paris for 3 weeks.
42. The people like to eat food.
43. May I have a drink or food?
44. Place the food on the table.
45. Give me directions of how I can find your house.
46. Something has been hidden in the house.
47. What is it?
48. Describe two hours of your life.
49. I can run as fast as Reza.
50. I can sing as loud as Emily.
51. Hello
52. My name is
53. How are you

54. Nice to meet you
55. Thank you.
56. Good bye
57. Getting up in the morning
58. Eating breakfast
59. Going to bed
60. Lighting the fire
61. Going down the shaft
62. I awake from sleep
63. I open my eyes
64. I look for my watch.
65. I find my watch
66. I see what time it is
67. It is six o'clock
68. I get out of bed
69. I put on my pants
70. I put on my stockings and shoes
71. I wash myself.
72. I comb my hair
73. I put on my collar and necktie
74. I go downstairs
75. I open the door of my bedroom.
76. We are getting warm
77. You are getting warm
78. They are getting warm
79. Mark wasn't driving, was he?
80. You weren't late, were you?

81. Excuse me for being late
82. I am sorry I am late.
83. I am sorry I forgot to come
84. (answer your letter)
85. Inform you
86. I had such a good time.
87. I hated to come back
88. Where were you last night?
89. What 'd you get so angry at me for this morning?
90. What is a warranty?
91. I just moved here
92. Don't be so picky, we can fix that
93. Marital status
94. Interests
95. Health
96. Community
97. How should children be punished for misbehavior?
98. What are your feelings about homework?
99. What psychologists call the "by stander effect" means?
100. That individuals are never willing to help out.

English

101. Discuss
102. Define
103. Talk about it = describe
104. A process
105. Concepts= description and summary

106. Of course
107. She answered all the questions
108. He jumps on the bus.
109. You ought to be more careful.
110. When the sea is calm, we will go out in a boat.
111. This story is more interesting than that.
112. I looked for my ruler but I can't find it.
113. They couldn't go by bus, so they went by train.
114. The weather was good, so the sea was calm.
115. It was his fault, because he wasn't very careful.
116. I can't cut the string because I haven't got a knife.
117. Cinema
118. To run away.
119. To run after
120. Whole
121. Please blow out that candle
122. He didn't put the money in his pocket.
123. I didn't buy my sister a watch
124. The dog didn't run after the cat.
125. He didn't give her a piece of chocolate.
126. He was beginning to help his mother.
127. The children were laughing and shouting.
128. We were buying flowers at the shop.
129. She picked up the coins
130. The dog led a blind man across the street.
131. No, I forgot nothing,
132. Never mind

133. Cheaper
134. I shall bring my things in a bag
135. He complained that it was cold.
136. Did you say that he was playing?
137. Lovely flower.
138. Will they buy a new car?
139. Will you come tomorrow?
140. Will he be very careful?
141. He looked everywhere for his hat.
142. Whistle
143. To take the penalty- kick.
144. Two goals to nothing.
145. You won't laugh when you hear this story.
146. We blow a whistle
147. He threw the ball through the window.
148. The bad man struck the policeman.
149. The cat was washing itself.
150. The nurse is tired because she has worked too hard.

Fish and Chips with Mushy Peas

Prep: 20 minutes
Cook: 40 minutes

Level: Intermediate
Yield: 4 servings

Ingredients

- One 10-ounce box frozen green peas
- 2 tablespoons cold unsalted butter
- Zest of 1 lemon
- Vegetable oil, for frying
- 2 pounds russet potatoes, peeled and cut into 1/3-inch-thick batons
- 2 cups all-purpose flour
- 1/2 cup rice flour
- 1 teaspoon baking soda
- 3/4 cup lager-style beer
- 3/4 cup seltzer or sparkling water
- 1 teaspoon lemon juice
- One 1 1/2-pound fillet hake, cut into 1 1/2-inch pieces (about 2 1/2 to 3 ounces each)
- Kosher salt and freshly ground pepper
- Malt vinegar, for serving

Preparation Directions

1. Bring 6 cups of generously salted water to a boil in a medium saucepan. Add the frozen peas and cook for 4 minutes. Reserve 3 tablespoons of the hot cooking water, and then drain the peas and return them to the pan. Immediately add the butter, lemon zest and cooking water and season with salt and pepper. Roughly mash the peas with a potato masher or in a food processor, and then cover and set aside.

2. Heat 2 inches of oil to 300 degrees F in a Dutch oven or heavy-bottomed wide pot. Meanwhile, rinse the potatoes with cold water to remove some of the surface starch and then dry well. Blanch the potatoes in 2 to 3 batches to avoid overcrowding the pot until just cooked through but still blond, about 2 minutes. Transfer to a paper-towel-lined baking sheet.

3. Raise the temperature of the oil to 345 degrees F. Preheat the oven to 200 degrees F. Whisk together 1 1/2 cups of the all-purpose flour, the rice flour, baking soda and 1 teaspoon salt. Pour in the beer, sparkling water and lemon juice and mix just until combined (do not over-mix). Keep the batter refrigerated until ready to use.

4. When the oil is ready, fry the potatoes in 2 to 3 batches until they are crisp and golden brown, about 3 minutes. Drain on a paper towel-lined baking sheet and sprinkle with salt, and then transfer to the oven to keep warm.

5. Sprinkle the fish fillets with salt and pepper. Coat the fish in the remaining all-purpose flour and then dip into the batter to completely coat. Carefully swish the fish partway into the oil for a few seconds before completely releasing. Once the coating starts to set on the first fillet, you can add another battered fillet into the oil. Fry until the fish is puffed, golden brown and cooked through, 5 minutes for thin fillets or 7 minutes for thick fillets, and then transfer to a paper towel-lined plate. Cook the remaining fillets and sprinkle with salt.

6. To serve, reheat the mushy peas if necessary. Serve the fish with the chips, mushy peas and malt vinegar on the side.

American Blueberry Pie:

Prep: 30 minutes

Cook: 40 minutes

Level: 240 minutes

Yield: 8 servings

English

Ingredients

- Double Crust Classic Crisco Pie Crust
- 7 cups peeled, cored, thinly sliced tart apples
- 1 cup fresh blueberries
- 1 tablespoon lemon juice
- 3/4 cup granulated sugar
- 1/4 cup firmly packed brown sugar
- 1/2 teaspoon ground cinnamon
- 1/2 teaspoon ground allspice
- 1/2 teaspoon ground nutmeg
- 2 tablespoons Pillsbury BEST™ All-Purpose Flour
- 1/2 tablespoon tapioca
- 2 tablespoons butter
- Glaze
- 1 large egg white
- 1/2 tablespoon warm water
- Sugar

Preparation Directions

1. Prepare recipe for double-crust pie, using a 9-inch pie plate. Roll out dough for bottom crust and place in pie plate according to recipe directions.

2. Heat oven to 425°F.

3. Toss apples and blueberries in a large bowl with lemon juice. Add granulated sugar, brown sugar, cinnamon, allspice, nutmeg, flour, and tapioca. Mix well. Spread evenly in prepared pie crust. Cut butter into small pieces and place on top of filling.

English

4. Roll out dough for top crust, place onto filled pie and finish edges according to pie crust recipe directions. Cut slits in top crust or prick with fork to vent steam.

5. Beat egg white with warm water. Brush on top crust. Sprinkle with sugar. Put a strip of foil around the edge of crust while baking to prevent excessive browning.

6. Bake 35 minutes. Remove foil; bake an additional 10 minutes or until crust is lightly golden and filling is bubbling.

Spanish:

1. Hola = Hello
2. Es'la disco = Table
3. Es'la Lampare = Lamp
4. Es'la Ventana = Window
5. No senor no es el televisor es el gato = No this is not a T.V., this is a cat
6. Es un lapis = pencil
7. Es un libro = This is a book
8. Es la pizarra = This is a black board
9. Es un Mapa = This is a map
10. Una Pluma = This is a pen
11. un papel = Paper
12. La clase = Class
13. el professor = professor, teacher.

14. Una mesa = student (m)
15. el muchacho = boy
16. una alumna = student (f)
17. una fruta = fruit
18. el avion = airplane
19. el cine = cinema
20. la cliente = customer
21. el pan = bread
22. el queso = cheeselas manzanas = apples
23. poco = little
24. las botellas de leche = a bottle of milk
25. el padre la television = man watching T.V.
26. los huevos = eggs
27. mucho = boy

Spanish

28. grande = elephant
29. bonito = beautiful
30. trabajador = construction labor worker
31. el aire = air
32. el ano = the year
33. la calle = the street
34. la cosa = the thing
35. el dinero = the money
36. la flor = the flower
37. el hombre = the man
38. la mujer = the woman
39. la oficina = the office

Spanish

40. el parquet = the park
41. la prisa = the hurry
42. la tienda = the store
43. alto, a = tall, high
44. extrano = strange
45. grande= big, large
46. mucho, a = a great deal
47. sus = their
48. tanto, a = so much
49. el cumpleanos = the birthday
50. Buenos dias = hello, good day
51. bien = well
52. adios = goodbye
53. tanto, a = so much
54. to dos, as, = every, all
55. tonto, a = foolish
56. mira = she looks, at watches
57. son = they are
58. van = they go, walk
59. visita = visitsvivir = to live
60. una = a
61. el chico usa el libro = the boy uses the book
62. vecino = the neighbor
63. el nene = the baby, el nino = the child
64. go zar = to enjoy
65. pobre = poor
66. ocupado, a = busy

67. su = his, her, your
68. comprar = to buy
69. escucnas = to listen
70. feliz = happy
71. dulces = candy
72. pagar = to pay
73. cocae = the car
74. el equipo = the team
75. amable = kind
76. la opportunidad = the opportunity
77. bello, a = beautiful
78. libre = free
79. el animal = the animal
80. la biblloteca = the library
81. el billete = the ticket
82. diego = james
83. gracias a dios! = Thank heaven! Thanks god

84. oir = to hear
85. cada = each
86. listo = ready
87. abierto, o = open
88. toda la famillia = the whole family
89. de papel = of paper
90. de vidrio = of glass
91. azul = blue
92. que = which, that

Spanish

93. la edad = the age
94. la hierba = the grassya = already
95. la ensalada de papas = the potato salad
96. volar = to fly
97. ilueve = it rains
98. mover = to move
99. al morzar = to lunch
100. nieva = it snows
101. elzapato = the shoe
102. la silla = the chair
103. la nariz = the nose
104. la escuela = the school
105. el future = the future
106. el idiota = the idiot
107. odiar = to hate
108. I pon! = put
109. la esposa = the wife
110. el risgo = the risk
111. la semana = the week
112. anda = you go, go
113. comprendo = understand
114. favorite, a = favorite
115. peligroso, a = dangerous
116. proximo, a = next
117. tanto = so much
118. escribir = to write
119. asi = such

120. juntos = together
121. sino = but
122. buen = good
123. el aceite = the oil
124. la esperanza = the hope
125. no importa = it doses not matter
126. el alma = the soul
127. la bodega = grocery store
128. tuve = had
129. al menos = at least
130. el Fuente = the fountain
131. de casados = as a married couple
132. morir = to die
133. tener mucha suerte = to be very lucky
134. ya no = not now, no langer
135. la piel = the skin
136. la fama = the fame
137. esperar = to wait
138. excusar = to excuse
139. suficiente = enough
140. si que = if that
141. to car = to play, music
142. acordado, a = remembered
143. mentir = to lie
144. Buenos dias = hello
145. Adios = goodbye

Chicken Tortilla Soup

Prep: 30 minutes
Cook: 30 minutes

Level: 40 minutes
Yield: 8 servings

Ingredients

- 6 corn tortillas (6 inches), divided
- 1-1/2 tsp. oil, divided
- 1/2 lb. boneless skinless chicken breasts, cut into bite-size pieces
- 2 cans (14-1/2 oz. each) chicken broth
- 1 cup TACO BELL® Thick & Chunky Medium Salsa
- 1 cup frozen corn
- 1 cup KRAFT Shredded Cheddar Cheese

Preparation Directions

1. Heat oven to 400°F.

2. Cut 2 tortillas into strips; toss with 1/2 tsp. oil. Spread in single layer on baking sheet. Bake 10 to 12 min. or until crisp, stirring occasionally.

3. Meanwhile, finely chop remaining tortillas. Heat remaining oil in large saucepan on medium-high heat. Add chicken; cook and stir 5 min. Add chopped tortillas, broth, salsa, and corn. Bring to boil; simmer on medium-low heat 15 min.

4. Serve topped with cheese and tortilla strips.

French:

1. Bonjour = Hello
2. Au revoir = goodbye
3. la babe = baby
4. le nom = name
5. le pere = father
6. le cousin = cousin
7. la niece = niece
8. la vie = life
9. le marriage = marriage
10. bruns = brown
11. raides = straight
12. e teint = complexion

13. blond = fair, blond
14. brun(e) = dark
15. rire = to laugh
16. figure = face
17. le nez = nose
18. la langue = tongue
19. le menton = chin
20. le corps = body
21. le bras = arm
22. la main = hand
23. talon = heel
24. la balcon = balcony

French

25. premier e'tage = first floor
26. le mur = wall
27. le garage = garage
28. le salon = living room
29. la table = table
30. le tapis = carpet
31. le cheminee = fireplace
32. la radio = radio
33. le four = oven
34. la gaz = gas
35. proper = clean
36. sale = dirty
37. la terre = soil
38. le nid = bird

39. le busson = bush
40. la tulipe = tulip
41. le bulbe = bulb
42. la rose = rose
43. la patte = paw
44. le lapin = rabbit
45. le bocal = bowl
46. la douche = shower
47. le savon = soap
48. nu(e) = naked
49. glace = mirror
50. se raser= to shave
51. la brosse = brush
52. le parfum = perfume
53. la cravate = tie
54. le tee = shirt = T- shirt
55. le chapeau = hat
56. les sandales = sandals
57. la balance = scales
58. la lampe de chavet = bedside lamp
59. le lit = bed
60. le bol = bowl
61. le pot = pitcher
62. le potage = soup
63. le dessert = dessert
64. le vin = wine
65. le bifteck = steak

66. le jambon = ham
67. la saucisse = sausage
68. la carotte = carrot
69. la tomate = tomato
70. cru(e) = raw
71. la salade = lettuce
72. le raisin = grapes
73. la fraise = strawberry
74. mur(e) = ripe
75. la prune = plum
76. le melon = melon
77. a mer or a mere = bitter, sharp

78. l' orange = orange
79. le yaourt = yogurt
80. le sel = salt
81. le riz = rice
82. les' epices = spices
83. la chocolat = chocolate
84. le biscuit = cookie
85. la patisserie = pastry
86. cuisine = cook
87. le disque = record
88. la musique classique = classical music
89. la journal = newspaper
90. le magazine = magazine
91. le journal illustre = comic magazine

French

92. la poe'sie = poetry
93. le tissue = fabric
94. la galerie = art gallery
95. la collection = collection
96. chanter = to sing
97. les jeux(m) = games
98. la place = seat
99. danser = to dance
100. le restaurant = restaurant
101. le garcon = waiter
102. commander= to order
103. le pour boire = tip
104. le plateau = tray
105. le zoo = zoo
106. l' addition = bill
107. le zebra = zebra
108. l' animal = animal
109. sauvage = wild
110. donner a manger = to feed
111. le gardien de zoo = zoo keeper
112. le parc = park
113. le pique- nique = picnic
114. le banc = bench
115. se reposer = to rest
116. le singe = monkey
117. le kangourou = kangaroo
118. le lion = lion

French

119. le tigre = tiger
120. le gardien = park keeper
121. la grande ville = city
122. la ville = town
123. pont = bridge
124. le cimetiere = cemetery
125. la pharmacie = pharmacy
126. le sac = bag
127. petit = small
128. moyen = medium
129. grand = large
130. combine coute = how much is
131. ca coute = it costs
132. l' escenseur = elevator
133. la letter = letter
134. le colis = package
135. collision = collision
136. capot= hood
137. le navire = ship
138. le pilote = pilot
139. les bagages a main = hand luggage
140. la pension = guest house
141. flotter = to float
142. moustique = mosquito
143. le bois = wood
144. la feuille = leaf
145. le chene = oak tree

French

146. le champ = field
147. le bureau = office
148. le representant de commerce = sale representative
149. en bonne sante = healthy
150. facile = easy/difficile = difficult

Beef Barley Soup

Prep: 15 minutes

Cook: 35 minutes

Level: 35 minutes

Yield: 6 servings

This hearty beef barley soup gets an added layer of flavor by the addition of cut-up cheese just at the end—it melts right in.

French

Ingredients

- 1/2 lb. ground beef
- 2-1/2 cups cold water
- 1 can (14-1/2 oz.) stewed tomatoes, cut up
- 3/4 cup sliced carrots
- 3/4 cup sliced mushrooms
- 1/2 cup quick-cooking barley, uncooked
- 2 cloves garlic, minced
- 1 tsp. dried oregano leaves
- 1/2 lb. (8 oz.) VELVEETA®, cut up

Preparation Directions

1. Brown meat in large saucepan; drain. Stir in water, tomatoes, carrots, mushrooms, barley, garlic, and oregano.

2. Bring to boil. Reduce heat to low; cover. Simmer 10 minutes or until barley is tender.

3. Add VELVEETA; stir until melted.

Italian:

1. Del pane = (some) bread
2. dello zucchero = sugar
3. della frutta = fruit
4. dell' acqua = water
5. dei bambini = children
6. delle case = houses
7. ho bisogno di soldi = I need some money
8. ho bisogno di amici = I need some friends
9. agni = each, every, all
10. l' inglese = languages

11. la bellezza = qualities
12. il generale = titles
13. I soldi sono utili = money is useful
14. lo ho dei soldi = I have some money
15. intelligenti = intelligent
16. ci sonodegli student nella classe = there are students in the classroom
17. io = I
18. Tu = You
19. Noi, lo = we
20. lui = he
21. lei = it
22. loro = they
23. lui m' ama = he loves me
24. lui l; ha vista = he saw her

Italian

25. miama, non mi ama = he loves me, he loves me not
26. maria compra I libri = Mary buys the book
27. maria li compra = Mary buys them
28. hai I biglietti = do you have the tickets
29. non li ho = I don't have them
30. lui ce lo mostra = he shows it to us
31. ne ha = Do you have some?
32. lui ne ha bisogno = he needs some.
33. il suo libro = her book
34. il libro di maria = Mary's book
35. le sue = his
36. le sue camicie = his shirts

37. una mia amica = a friend of mine
38. un tuo libro = a book of yours
39. si, e' mia = yes, it is mine
40. mi vesto = I get dressed
41. vesto mio figlio = I dress my son
42. ti, t' = yourself
43. mi lavo il viso = I wash my face
44. mi lavo = I wash myself
45. chi e? I o! = who is it?
46. sei tu! = It is you!
47. vuoi una mano? = Can I help you?
48. no grazie, faccio da me = no thanks, I 'll do it
49. chie' ansioso? I o = who is worried? I am
50. chi arriva? Noi. = Who is coming? We are.
51. I figli di maria stanno studianda quelli di silvia guardano la telvisione = Mary's kids are studying, Silvia's are watching T.V.

Italian

52. lui e' quello che amo = he is the one I love
53. bianco = white
54. largo = big
55. rosa = pink
56. viola = purple
57. blu = blue
58. qualche = some
59. qualsiasi = any
60. meglio = better
61. una vecchia amica = an old friend

Italian

62. un acara amica = a dear friend
63. minore, il minore = smaller, the smallest
64. cattivo peggio, il peggiore = worse, the worst
65. grande- maggiore- il maggiore = greater, bigger
66. questa casa qui molto grande = this house is really big
67. quella macchina la' e vecchia = that car is old.
68. mio fratello si chiama franco = my brother's name is Frank
69. suo padre viaggia molto = her father travels a lot
70. piacere mio = my pleasure
71. quanti libri hai = How many books do you have?
72. che ora e' = what time is it?
73. che bella casa hai = What a beautiful house you have
74. che compito abbiamo per domain? = What homework do we have for tomorrow?
75. Primo = president
76. non so che fare = I wonder what to do.
77. gli student vengono da lute le parti = the students come from all around
78. ieri = when
79. qui = where
80. molto = how
81. non vedo nessuno = I don't see anybody.
82. non ho ne' tempo ne' denaro = I have neither time nor money
83. suona il piano Giovanni? = Does John play the piano?
84. canta bene maria? = does Mary sing well?
85. Cantante = singer
86. Ambulante = walking
87. eguente = following
88. il gatto = cat

89. soprovvissuti = the survivors
90. il primo venuto = the first to arrive
91. il cane = dog
92. I fiori = flower
93. la posta = mail
94. la moto = motor
95. la bicicletta = la bici = bicycle
96. grigio = gray
97. giallo = yellow
98. nero = black
99. orancione = orange
100. I colori = colors
101. biglietti = paper money
102. monete (moh-neh- the) = money change
103. mattina (math-tee-nah) = morning
104. pomeriggio (poh-meh-ree-joh) = afternoon
105. sera (she- rah) = evening
106. la note = night
107. il caffe = coffee
108. il te' = tea
109. il pane = bread
110. il pepe = pepper
111. il sale = salt
112. la Chiesa (kee-eh- zah) = church
113. il metallo = metal
114. il metro = meter

115. milione = million
116. la misura (mee- zoo-rah) = measure, size
117. la moda = style, fashion
118. il museo = museum
119. il momento = moment
120. la montagna = mountain
121. native = native
122. necessario = necessary
123. nuovo = new
124. nord = north
125. normale = normal
126. l' ombrello = umbrella
127. l' ospedale = hospital
128. Ovest = west
129. il paio = pair
130. il palazzo = palace, building
131. perfetto = perfect
132. il permesso = permission
133. sud = south
134. est = east
135. la polizia = police
136. povero = poor
137. la porta = door
138. il prezzo(preh-tsoh) = price
139. il problema = problem
140. pronto = prompt = ready
141. pronto! = Hello(telephone)

142. la qualita = quality
143. Signore = ladies, women
144. Signori = men
145. Ricco = rich
146. il rispetto = respect
147. serio = serious
148. simile = similar
149. la somma = total, sum
150. primo = first
151. ama = love

Four-Cheese Lasagna

Prep: 30 minutes

Cook: 40 minutes

Level: 70 minutes

Yield: 12 servings

Wondering what kinds of cheese show up in this lasagna? You can count on Neufchatel, cottage cheese, mozzarella, and Parmesan to make an appearance.

Italian

Ingredients

- 1 lb. extra-lean ground beef 1 lb for $4.99 thru 03/01
- 1 onion, chopped
- 1 pkg. (8 oz.) PHILADELPHIA Neufchatel Cheese, softened
- 1 cup BREAKSTONE'S or KNUDSEN 2% Milkfat Low Fat Cottage Cheese
- 1 pkg. (8 oz.) KRAFT Shredded Low-Moisture Part-Skim Mozzarella Cheese, divided
- 1/2 cup KRAFT Grated Parmesan Cheese, divided
- 1 egg, beaten
- 1 jar (24 oz.) CLASSICO FAMILY FAVORITES Traditional Pasta Sauce
- 1 can (14.5 oz.) diced tomatoes, drained
- 1/2 tsp. dried oregano leaves
- 12 lasagna noodles, cooked

Preparation Directions

1. Heat oven to 350°F.

2. Brown meat with onions in large skillet. Meanwhile, mix Neufchatel, cottage cheese, 1-1/2 cups mozzarella, 1/4 cup Parmesan and egg until blended.

3. Drain meat; return to skillet. Stir in pasta sauce, tomatoes, and oregano; simmer 5 min. Remove from heat. Spoon 1 cup meat sauce onto bottom of 13x9-inch baking dish; top with layers of 3 lasagna noodles, 1 cup cheese mixture and 1 cup meat sauce. Repeat layers twice. Top with remaining noodles, meat sauce, mozzarella, and Parmesan; cover.

4. Bake 50 min. or until heated through, uncovering after 40 min. Let stand 10 min. before cutting to serve.

Chinese:

1. bu'cuo' = pretty good
2. duo' = more, many
3. ga'o = tall, high
4. danshi = but
5. shao = less, few
6. yaobu(ra'n) = otherwise
7. lia'ng = cool
8. le = new situation
9. e' = hungry
10. bie' = don't
11. la'o = old
12. y'ou = both and

Chinese

13. ca'ise = color
14. bu le = not anymore
15. hui = to return
16. zhi' = only
17. du' shu = to study
18. he' = and
19. ma'n = slow
20. me'n = door
21. hua'yua'n = garden
22. shu(ke) = tree
23. shu'ca'I = vegetables
24. shafa = sofa

Chinese

25. beizi = cup
26. tang = sugar
27. chazuo = socket
28. We'ibo'lu = microwave
29. hua'cha' = jasmine tea
30. Ce'suo' = toilet
31. ya'shua' = toothbrush
32. nianji = age
33. shenti = health, body
34. huo' = good
35. pia'nyi = cheap
36. de'ng = etc.
37. bufen = part, section
38. ba'okuo = to include

39. shengyi = business
40. shebei = equipment, facilities
41. chengre'n = to admit
42. mo'u = certain
43. gonggong = public
44. ha'o = good, he'n ha'o = very good
45. zui ha'o = the best
46. zhengcha'ng = normal, regular
47. luxing = to travel
48. yin = cloudy, overcast
49. na'nnu' = men and women
50. la'oshao = old and young
51. na'n = difficult
52. ge'n = with, and
53. yiqi = together
54. fa'nzheng = any way, in any case
55. da'o qu/la'I = to go/ come to/ to arrive
56. yua'n = palace
57. qingchu = clear, clearly
58. a shi a da'nshi = it's a all right but
59. you yisi = to be interesting
60. mu' = eye
61. si' = silk
62. shi' = food
63. ma' = horse
64. ni'ao = bird
65. bing = ice

66. yo'u = also, again
67. cu'n = inch
68. he'ng = horizontal
69. shu' = vertical
70. tian = field
71. cho'ng = insect
72. yu' = rain
73. gu' = bone
74. he'i = black, dark
75. yu' = feather/wing
76. sho'u = hand
77. huo' che' = train
78. weixia'n = danger
79. ta'o = set
80. ba'o = newspaper
81. fe'n = a copy
82. wa'iguo' = foreign
83. ba'n = half
84. me'I = not
85. zaijia'n = goodbye
86. tu = earth
87. ya'o = want
88. qu' = to go
89. yue' = month
90. ha'I = still
91. ni' = you
92. dianying = film
93. ge' = see

Chinese

94. ya'n = speech
95. mu' = eye
96. re'n = person
97. da'o = knife
98. shu' = vertical (line)
99. tia'n = field
100. zhuanjia = expert
101. ma'I = to sell
102. ca'o = grass
103. shui' = water
104. xin = heart
105. e'r = ear
106. shi = food
107. we'n lu' = ask the way
108. yuan = far
109. ji'n = near
110. zhongguo ge'ming bowuguan = museum of revolution- china revolution.
111. Defang = place
112. Xin = letter
113. zho'ng = heavy
114. hangkong = airmail
115. pingxin = surface mail
116. xian = first
117. tie'(shang) = to stick (on)
118. dizhi = address
119. shouju = receipt
120. guitai = counter
121. we'I shenme = why
122. ding = top, peak

123. rilluo = sunset
124. xiwang = to hope
125. shi = poem
126. do'u = funny
127. wa'ng = to forget
128. diu' = to lose
129. huaiyi = to suspect
130. wenti = question, problem
131. ge'ge' = each, every
132. zu' = to rent, hire
133. zhiye' = occupation, fresh
134. ga'njue' = feeling, sense
135. xinxian = fresh
136. tongyi = to agree with
137. feng = wind
138. ding = to go against
139. duo = how
140. gudian = classical
141. tian = sweet
142. likai = to leave
143. liwu = present, gift
144. haha = haha
145. youyi = friendship
146. zui = drunk
147. hong = red
148. kuaile = happy, joyful

Beef and Vegetable Stir-Fry

Prep: 25 minutes

Cook: 25 minutes

Level: 30 minutes

Yield: 4 servings

Very good! Will make this again! Great and quick! (Those are just a few of the accolades this beef stir-fry has received from cooks like you.)

Ingredients

- 1/4 cup lite soy sauce
- 2 Tbsp. KRAFT Lite CATALINA Dressing
- 3/4 tsp. ground ginger
- 1 lb. beef flank steak, cut into thin strips
- 1 pkg. (16 oz.) frozen stir-fry vegetables, thawed, drained
- 1/4 cup PLANTERS Dry Roasted Peanuts

Preparation Directions

1. Cook rice as directed on package, omitting salt.

2. Meanwhile, mix soy sauce, dressing and ginger until blended; set aside. Toss meat with cornstarch; cook and stir in large nonstick skillet sprayed with cooking spray on medium-high heat 3 min. or until done. Add vegetables and soy sauce mixture; cook and stir 3 min. or until sauce is thickened and vegetables are heated through.

3. Spoon over rice; top with nuts.

German:

1. guten morgen = good morning
2. guten abend = good evening
3. gute nacht = good night
4. auf wiedersehen = goodbye
5. sind sie aus Manchester? = are you from Manchester?
6. arbeiten sie onne computer? = Are you working with your computer?
7. haben sie sechs kinder? = Do you have six children?
8. fliegen sie nach berlin? = flying to Berlin?
9. Zimmer = room
10. haben sie jetzt mehr geld? = Now you have more money?
11. Zu = too = night

German

12. Teuer = expensive
13. 14-bath = bed
14. Dushe = shower
15. Hier = here
16. Links = left
17. Genug = enough
18. Klein = small
19. nur = only
20. fru'hstu'ck = breakfast
21. von = from
22. bis = until
23. halb = half
24. tee = tea
25. oder = or
26. vor = before
27. café' = café
28. dann = then
29. essen = eat
30. einmal = once
31. tisch = table
32. gehen = go
33. heute = today
34. zentrum = center
35. bus = bus
36. es tut mir leid = I am sorry
37. alle = all
38. fussball = football

German

39. koffer = suitcase
40. neu = new
41. ach, du meine gute = good grief!
42. Glauben = ich glaube = believe, I believe
43. Spatter = later
44. Zuviel = too much stuck = piece
45. Brot = bread
46. ei, eier = egg, eggs
47. bier = beer
48. tu'te = bag
49. mich = me
50. genau = exactly grosse = size
51. wer = who
52. net = nice
53. billig = cheap
54. wolle = wool
55. baum wolle = cotton
56. zeitung = newspaper
57. sagen = say, said
58. warum = why auf = on
59. papier = paper
60. bei, beim = at, at the
61. buch = book
62. kennen = to know
63. ihn, ihm = him
64. termin = appointment
65. sache = matter, thing

66. danke = thank you
67. sicher = sure, certainly
68. naturlich = of course
69. interessant = interesting
70. zeit = time
71. wunderbar = wonderfulein paar= a few
72. arzt = doctor
73. krank = sick
74. ach so = I see
75. oben = at the top
76. an = at
77. ausgang = exit
78. tur = door
79. vielen dank = thank you very much
80. hinter = behind
81. kirche = church
82. gemu'tlich = comfortable
83. unser'e = our
84. hund = dog
85. schmerzen = pains
86. kommen = come
87. eis = icecream
88. huhn = chicken
89. gemu'se = vegetables
90. obst = fruit
91. wasser = water
92. fertig = ready

93. niemand = nobody
94. lieber = rather, prefer
95. brat wurst = fried sausage
96. unter wegs = on the move
97. fahr karte = ticket
98. zug = train
99. rauchen = to smoke
100. ver boten = forbidden
101. brief = letter
102. kasten = box
103. foto = photo
104. see = lake, sea
105. beide = both

Gerrman

106. voll = full
107. zweimal = twice
108. weil = because
109. alt = old
110. hoffen = to hope
111. dass = that
112. erste = first
113. letzte = last
114. thank stele = gas station
115. schule = school
116. u-bahn = underground
117. ampel = traffic light
118. wenn = if, when

119. uns = us
120. heiss = hot
121. flug hafen = airport
122. leute = people
123. mutter = mother
124. wie geht's? = how are you?
125. richtig = right
126. wohnen = live
127. sein = his
128. junge = boy
129. schreiben = write
130. nie = never
131. flug = flight
132. was ist los? = what is the matter?
133. A = yes
134. flugzeug = airplane
135. wir = we
136. bitte = please
137. entschldigen sie = excuse me
138. sind = are
139. gutten tag = hello, good day
140. nein = no
141. leider = unfortunately
142. nicht = not
143. stadt = town, city
144. sher = very
145. fur = for, mehr = more geld = money

Roasted Cheese Bagel Bites

Prep: 20 minutes

Cook: 34 minutes

Level: 14 minutes

Yield: 3 servings

German

Ingredients

- 1 box (9 ct.) Three Cheese Bagel Bites®
- 1 jar pitted Kalamata olive
- 1 jar roasted red peppers

Preparation Directions

1. Preheat oven to 425°F.

2. Dice the olives. Chop roasted red peppers. Remove tomatoes from oil and chop.

3. Remove bagels from package. Top each bagel with olives, red peppers, and tomatoes. Bake at 425°F for 14 mins. Remove from oven, plate, and serve.

Farsi:

1. Abort = aghim
2. a bomb = bomb
3. absent = ghayeb
4. accuracy = deghat
5. accustom = addat kardam
6. acknowledge = shenakhtan
7. addiction = e'tyadd
8. adult = balegh
9. a fire = ah'tash
10. alarm – clock = sah'hat
11. ally = dost

Farsi

12. amaze = ta'ajob kardan
13. a miss = nah'dorost
14. arrest = das'gir
15. arsenic = margeh' mosh
16. auction = hara'j
17. author = nevie'sandeh
18. awesome = mayeh hormat
19. baby = bat'cheh
20. bait = toh'meh, azyat kardan
21. barbecue = kabab kardan
22. bashful = tar'so
23. bastard = harom' zadeh
24. bath = shosteh' sho kardan
25. battle = nabbard
26. beggar = geh'da
27. bet = shart'bandi
28. blind = koor
29. blowzy = sheh'lakhteh
30. boss = ray'eiss
31. bow = kham'shodan
32. briefly = mokh'tasar
33. broker = dal'lal
34. buyer = khari'dar
35. butter = kar'eh
36. capital = sar'mayeh
37. chef = ash'paz
38. chop-house = restaurant = restaurant arzaan

Farsi

39. citizenship = tah'bahi'yat
40. complex = peh' chi'deh
41. console = del'dari daddan
42. construction = sah'khteman sazzi
43. conviction = mah'ko'mi'yat
44. cottage = kol'beh
45. dangerous = kha'tar'nock
46. dead = mor'deh
47. despite = eh' ha'nat
48. disloyalty = bie' vaf'ie

Farsi

49. distinction = far'gh, emtiyaz
50. down pour = baran'degi zyaad
51. ear = gosh
52. eat = khor'dan
53. ensure = beh dast avardan
54. encore = do' bareh
55. enough = an'daazeh
56. baba = father
57. baba aob daad = father give a water
58. koja meri = where are you going?
59. halet chetor = how are you?
60. mie khari = buying
61. del = heart
62. dass = hand
63. feet = paa
64. an'gosht = finger

65. san'dalli = chair
66. miez = table
67. zamine = earth
68. khah'k = soil
69. keeh'ream = lotion
70. nah ghashi = paint
71. ghorse = pills, medicine
72. mehmaar = architect
73. rah randeh = drivers
74. pan'jareh = window
75. daar = door
76. farsh = rug
77. ceh' ragh = lamp
78. telephone = phone
79. exam = e'mteh'han
80. excretion = annn = , madfu
81. fag = jon moft kanden
82. falsely = do'roghi
83. fat = chagh
84. feeling = e'h'sas
85. fine = jar'rimeh
86. fishy = mash'kok
87. flower = gool
88. floor = kaff' otagh
89. fly = mah'gass
90. force = zoor
91. fountain = fah'fareh

92. free = azaad
93. frozen = e'akhzadeh
94. fuzzy = na' malom
95. game = baize
96. gather = jam kardan
97. geography = goghrafi
98. way = rah
99. good = khoob
100. grass = cha'man
101. half = nes'f
102. hat = koh'lah
103. almond = ba'dam
104. walnuts = ger'do
105. psychology = ravan shenasi
106. dentist = dandan pe'zeshk
107. independent = es'tegh'lal
108. tree = de'rakht

109. kiss = boos
110. chess = shat'ranj
111. lawyer = va'kill
112. landlord = sa'heb'khoneh
113. leaf = ba'rg
114. left = chap
115. right = roust
116. like = mes'leh
117. lunch = na' har

Farsi

118. dinner = sham
119. make-up = aarh'yesh
120. map = nagh'sheh
121. miss = az dast dadan
122. money = pool
123. monkey = may'mon
124. numbers = shomareh
125. oil = ro'ghan
126. office = daftar
127. part = e' ghesmat
128. passion = hayeh'jon
129. pieb = sherini
130. perfect = ka'mail
131. race = mo'sa'begheh
132. rent = e'h'ja'reh
133. roof = sa'ghf
134. round = ge'rd
135. salt = na'mak
136. save = nehjot
137. screw = pe'ch
138. seat = jah, sandalli
139. a man of sense = e'nsan e'h ba sho'ore
140. shoe = ka' fe'sh
141. sleep = khaab
142. slow = ah' hesteh
143. spring = bahar
144. stone = sang

Farsi

145. tooth = dan'daon
146. under = zieer
147. ugly = zehsht
148. pot = dieeg

White Rice

Prep: 5 minutes

Cook: 40 minutes

Level: Immmediate

Yield: 5 servings

Farsi

Ingredients

- 3 cups basmati or long-grain rice
- 8 cups water
- 2 tablespoons vegetable oil
- 1/2 teaspoon salt

Preparation Direction

1. Wash rice in cold water. Drain and place in large bowl. Add about 8 cups of warm water. Allow to sit for 2-3 hours covered.

2. After rice has soaked, drain, and save 6 cups of the water.

3. Pour rice water into a medium saucepan and bring to a boil. Add rice and salt. Allow to cook for about 10 minutes. Remove rice from heat and drain.

4. Pour vegetable oil in bottom of saucepan, add rice, then 2 tablespoons of vegetable oil on top. Simmer on low for 20 minutes or until rice is done.

Japanese:

1. what time is it? = Nan- ji desu ka? (nahn- jee dess-kah?)
2. It is five-thirty = Go- ji- han desu = (Go-jee- Hahn- dess)
3. What time do you leave? Nan- Ji Ni demass- Ka? (nahn-jee-nee-day-mahss-kah?)
4. I have no more time? = Moh ji- kan ga nai desu? (Moe-jee- khan gah-nie-dess?)
5. Do we still have time? = Mada ji- kan ga arimass ka? (Mah-da –jee khan gah ah-ree- mahss-kah?)
6. 1 day = ichi-nichi (e- chee- nee- chee)
7. I am going to stay two days = futsuka-kan tomarimass- (futes-kah-kahn toe mah- ree-mahss)
8. What day is today? = Kyo wa nan yobi desu ka? (k'yoe wah nahn yoe-bee dess kah)
9. I hate Mondays = watakushi wa getsuyobi ga kiraidesu = (wah- tock-she wah gate- sue- yoe-bee gah kee rye dess.)

10. But I love Fridays. = keredomo, kinyobi ga suki desu. = (kay- ray-doe-moe, keen, yoe –bee-gah ski dess.
11. Next year I am going to Japan = rai nen ninon e ikimasu. (rye nane nee- hone eh ee kee mahs.)
12. Please sign your name here = koko de namae wo kaite kudasai = (koe-koe day nah- my oh kite-tay kuu-dah-sie.)
13. Are you Mr. Watanabe? = Anata wa watanabe- san desu ka?
14. We = watakushi- tachi- (wah- tock-she-tah-chee)
15. You = anata-tachi(ah-nah-tah-tah-chee)
16. Who? = Donate? (doe-nah-tah)
17. Who is it? = Donate desu ka?
18. what is it? = nan desu ka?
19. itsu (eet-sue?)
20. what do you want to eat? = Nani wo ta be tai no desu ka?
21. where? = do ko? (doe- koe?)
22. where are you going? = Doko e iki masu ka?
23. where is it = doko ni a ri masu ka?
24. Yes = hai(hie)
25. No = lie(ea-eh)
26. Hello = moshi-moshi
27. thank you = ariguto gozaimasu
28. thank you very much = domo arigato gozaimasu (doe- moe ah-ree-gah-toe –go-zie-mahss)
29. don't mention it. = do I tah shi mashite (doe-ee-tah-she-mahssh-tay)
30. excuse me = sum imasen! (sue- me- mah-sin)
31. Welcome = irrashaimase (ee-rah-shy-mah-say)
32. good morning = ohaiyo gozaimasu (oh-hie-yee-go-zie-mahss)
33. good night = oyasumi nasai
34. excuse me = I'am sorry = go me na sai
35. just a moment, please = chotto matte kudasai

36. It's hot, isn't it! = Atusui desu, ne!
37. What time is it? = Nan- ji desu Ka?
38. How are you? = O' genki desu ka?
39. Genki desu = I am fine.
40. Do you speak English? = Eigo ga hanasemasu ka?
41. I understand a little = Sukoshi wakarimasu
42. Please wait here = Koko de matte kudasai
43. I am the bus driver = watakushi ga basu no untenshu desu
44. please get ready quickly = Hayaku yoi shite kudasai.
45. show me your passport, please = pasupoto wo misete kudasai
46. are you here on business? = Shigoto de kimashita ka?
47. how many (pieces) do you have? = Ikutsu arimasu ka?
48. that's fine. Thank you = kekko desu. Domo arigat
49. shall I help you? = Tetsudai masho ka? (tate- sue-die mah-show-kah?)
50. where do you want to go? = Doko e ikitai no desu ka?

51. head = atama(ah-tah-mah)
52. ear = mimi(me-me)
53. eyebrows = mayuge(mah-yuu-gay)
54. eye = me(may)
55. nose = hana(hana)
56. lips = kuchibiru
57. Neck = kubi(kun-bee)
58. Hand = te(tay)
59. Finger = yubi (yuu- bee)
60. Leg = ashi

Japanese

61. Heart = Shinzo(sheen-zoe)
62. Liver = kanzo(kahn-zoe)
63. Kidney = jinzo
64. Rear = o' shiri = back
65. Apple = ringo(reen-go)
66. Stomach ache = onaka ga itai (oh-nah- kah-gahe-tie)
67. Chicken = chikin
68. Eggs = tamago
69. Garlic =ninniku
70. Grape = budo
71. green peas = gurin pisu
72. salt = shio
73. mustard = masutado
74. rice = gohan(go-hahn)
75. onion(s) = tamanegi (tah- mah- nay-ghee)
76. sugar= sato
77. soup = supu
78. toast = tosuto
79. vegetables = yasai(yah-sie)
80. spoon = supunn (su- punne)
81. fork = foku
82. knife = naifu(nie-fuu)
83. beer = biru
84. coca-cola = koka kora
85. milk = miruku(mee-rue-kuu)
86. this way please = dozo, kochira e (doe-zoe-koe- chee-rah-eh)
87. the bill please = okanjo kudassai

88. address = jusho(juu-show)
89. age = toshi
90. adult = otona
91. admission fee = nyujo ryo
92. air-conditioner = reibo
93. airport = kuko
94. all right(ok) = dai jobu
95. alone = hitori
96. answer = henji (hane- jee) 98- a partment = apato
97. appetizer = zensai (zen- sigh)
98. arrang (get ready) = junbi(junne-bee)
99. arrival gate = tochaku geito
100. as soon as possible = narube ku hayaku
101. oba- san (oh-bah- sahn)
102. back(of/behind) = ushiro
103. bad = warui (wah-rue-e)
104. bad(taste) = mazui(mah-zuu-ee)
105. bag = bagu(bah-guu)
106. baggage = nimotsu
107. bank = ginko
108. bar = baa(baah)
109. barber = tokoya
110. bargain sale = oyasu uri
111. basement = chika (chee- kah)
112. big= okii(oh-keee)
113. big car = ogata sha
114. blood pressure = ketsu atsu

115. book = hon(hone)
116. bread = pan
117. cash = genkin(gain-keen)
118. change(money) = o' tsuri (oh- t'-sue-ree)
119. channel (T.V.) = chaneru(chah-nay-rue)
120. cheap = yasui(yah-sue-ee)
121. cheese = chizu
122. chicken = niwatori(nee-wah-toe-ree)
123. child = kodomo
124. food = ryori
125. city = shi
126. clock = watch = tokei(toe-kay-e)
127. close = shut = shimemasu(she-may-mahss)
128. deliver = todokemasu
129. early = hayai(hah-yie)
130. eat = tabemasu(tah-bay-mahss)
131. electricity = light = denki(dane-kee)
132. embassy = taishikan
133. elevator = erebeta
134. enjoy = tanoshimimasu
135. evening = yagata(yuu-gah-tah)
136. expense = hiyo (he-yoe)
137. fairway = feauei(fay-ah-way)
138. dream = yume
139. far = toi(toy)
140. girl = onna = nook
141. foreign = gaikoku no(guy-ko-kuu-no)

142. free (no cost) = muryo(muu-rio)
143. gloves = tebukuro(tay-bua-kuu-roe)
144. headache = zutsu shimasu
145. hospital = byooin(b'-yohn-een)
146. husband = shujin
147. interesting = omoshiroi(oh-moe-she-roy)
148. jewelry = hohseki(hoeh-say-kee)

Arabic:

1. I = anaa
2. You = anta
3. He = huwa
4. They = umaa
5. we = nahnu
6. they(m) = hum(hamm)
7. first name = al –ism
8. Sex(m)(f) = al jins
9. place of birth = makaan al- wilaada
10. marital status = al- haala al- madaniyya
11. single = a' zab

12. Married = mutazawwij
13. Passport = jawaaz safar
14. what day is it today? = Maa- I – yawm
15. tonight= haadhihi al- Layla (hazat –al- lyyla)
16. next = al- qaadim (Ghadem)
17. 1st = al awwa
18. 2nd = ath- thaani (ath- sunni)
19. On = ala
20. Is it going to rain? = Hal satumtir
21. Downpour = gha aim
22. what's the weather going to be like today/ tomorrow? = kayfa sayakuun at tags al-/yawm
23. between and = bain Wa
24. middle = wasat
25. here/ there = hunaa/ hunaak
26. every where = fii kul makaan
27. under = tahta
28. near = qurba
29. in front of = amaama
30. up = fawq
31. inside = daakhil
32. outside = khaarij
33. behind = khalf
34. at the front = fii al muqaddima
35. in the north = fii ash – shamaal
36. south = januub

37. west = gharb
38. east = sharq
39. push = idfa
40. hotel = funduq
41. information = maluumaat
42. police = shurta
43. full = mamluu
44. danger = khatar
45. hello = ahlan
46. welcome = marhabar
47. how are you? = kayfa haaluk?
48. good luck = hazzan saiidan
49. thank you = shukran
50. say hello to all = sallim alaa kum
51. who? = man?
52. What? = maadhaa(ma'za)
53. what is this? = Maa haadhaa
54. where? = ayna
55. which one? = ay waahid
56. when? = Mataa?
57. where are you going? = illaa ayna anta dhaahib (dh=z)
58. why? = limaadhaa
59. could you? = hal yumkin min fadlik?
60. do you have? = Hal laday kum?
61. Sure = akiid
62. Yes, of course = na am, taban
63. alright = tamaam

64. perhaps = rubbamaa
65. no problem = laa mushkila
66. that's all right = laysat mushkila
67. never mind/ forget it = laa tahtam/ insa dhaalik (dh=z)
68. well done! = ahsanta sun'an
69. not bad = laa basai
70. how awful = yaa lahu min a mrin kariih
71. I am fed up = anaa munzaij
72. this is no good = haadhaa laysa jayyidan
73. friend = sadiiq
74. I am single = anaa a'zab
75. Flag = alam
76. I work in an office = a' mal fill maktab
77. Food = ta'aam
78. Forget = yansaa
79. Free = hur (un occupied)
80. Fresh = taazij
81. Fruit = fawaakih
82. Frozen = mujammad
83. Gallery = bahw (saala)
84. Gasoline = benzin
85. Glass = zujaaj
86. grandfather = jadgrilled = mashwii
87. grocer = baqqaal
88. hand = yad
89. hat = qubba'a
90. heal = yasma

91. heart = qalb
92. heat = haraara
93. heel (of shoe) = ka'b
94. here = hunaa
95. hire = yastajir
96. holiday = u tia(uot'let)
97. how long = kam al mudda
98. jack (for car) = raafia
99. jaw = fak
100. jewelry = mujawharaat
101. job = shughl = wazifa
102. juice = asiir
103. knife = sikiin
104. know = ya'rif

105. ladder = daraj
106. land = ard (arz)
107. line = khat
108. local = mahallii
109. loss = fiqdaan = khasaara
110. loud = aalin
111. love = hub = yuhib
112. low = munkhafid
113. lunch = ghidhaa(qaza)
114. market = suuq
115. mat (on floor) = sajaada
116. mayor = muhaafiz

117. mean = yanii
118. meat = lahm
119. new = jadiid
120. mouth = fam
121. monkey = qird
122. money = nuquud
123. nose = anf
124. nuts = fustuq
125. okay = naam
126. open = maftuuh
127. page = safha
128. pane = lawh
129. pan = miqlaat
130. pen = galam
131. password = kalimat-al- ser
132. people = naas
133. pills, tablets = hubuub
134. playing cards = al waraq
135. pond = birka
136. potato = bataatis
137. photo = suura(sorat)
138. pulse = nabd(nabz)
139. pure = naqii
140. rain = ma tar
141. raw = khaam
142. really = haqqan
143. red = ahmar

Arabic

144. scales = mizaan
145. shoe = hidhaa(hiza)
146. shop = yatasawwaq
147. sleep = yanaam
148. size = hajm
149. walk = mashie imshi

Russian:

1. Good morning = Dobroye o'tra
2. good day = Dobry dyen
3. good evening = dobry vyecher
4. hello = zdrgstvooeetye
5. goodbye = Da sveedanya
6. I am called = Minya zavoot
7. please to meet you = Ochen preey atna
8. what are you called? = Kak vas zavoot?
9. How are things? = Kak dyila?
10. good well = Kharasho

Russian

11. excuse me/ I am sorry = eezveeneetye maladoy
12. you = Vy
13. no = nyet
14. I = ya
15. Not = nye
16. Yes = Da
17. young woman/ miss = Dyevushka
18. we = Mbi
19. He = Oh
20. I don't understand = Yan ye paneemayoo
21. slower please = Myedlyn- ye- ye- pazhal- sta
22. I speak Russian badly = Ya gavaryoo pa- roosky plokha
23. You (several persons) = Bbi
24. She = Oha'
25. You = Tbi (1 person)
26. I = R> (R in other direction)
27. over there = von tam
28. cinema = keenotigtr
29. information office = spragvuchnoye
30. don't mention it = nye za shto!
31. c sound like s in = sit
32. p sound like r in = rabbit
33. e sound like ye = in yesterday
34. b sound like v in = visitor
35. h sound like n in = note
36. y sound like oo in = boot
37. co'yc = savce (sound)

Russian

38. kakao = cocoa
39. rum = pom
40. sugar = caxap
41. red = krasny
42. white = byely
43. yellow = zholty
44. green = zilyony
45. black = chorny
46. go = eedeetye
47. how do you get to the center? = kak papast v? T sentr
48. straight ahead = pryam ei
49. interesting = intiryesny
50. closed = zakryt
51. for repairs = na rimont
52. oh, what a pity = kak zhal
53. aim = tsel
54. alive = zhivoy
55. all = vyes
56. angry = sirdity
57. art = isku'stva
58. ask = sprashivat, prasit
59. back = spina
60. bag = su'mka, mishok
61. bath = vana
62. bed = kravat
63. beer = piva
64. begin = nachinati

65. believe = palagat
66. best = luchshiy
67. bicycle = vilasipyet
68. blue = galuboy
69. blood = krof
70. born = razhdyony
71. bowl = miska
72. boy = malchik
73. brake = tarmazit
74. brand = fabrichnaya marka
75. bread = khlyep
76. bright = yarkly
77. brother = brat
78. build = stroyit
79. burn = zhar- azhok
80. bus = aftobus
81. butter = masla
82. cake = pirok
83. car = mashyna
84. care = zabota
85. careful = astarozhny
86. carpet = kavyo'r
87. chair = stul
88. cheap =dishovy
89. cheese = syr
90. chess = shakhmaty
91. chicken = ku'ritsa

Russian

92. child = ribyonok
93. choice = vybor
94. choose = vybirat
95. Christmas = razhdyestvo
96. Circus = tsyrk
97. Citizen = grazhdanin
98. City = go'rat
99. Clean = chisty
100. Clock = chisy
101. Client = kliyent
102. Closet = shkaf
103. Clothes = adyezhda
104. Cloud = oblaka
105. Compare = sravnivat
106. Cool = prakhladny
107. Condition = usloviye
108. Consist = sastayat'
109. Cost = tsina
110. Cow = karova
111. Craft = rimislo
112. Crazy = sumashedshy
113. Crime = pryestuplyeniye
114. Culture = kultura
115. Cut = paryes,
116. Cat = ryezat
117. Dad = papa dairy(story) malochny magazine
118. Danger = apasnast

Russian

119. Dead = myortvy
120. Decide = risha't'
121. Divorce = razvod
122. Drawing = risunok
123. Excellent = privaskhodny
124. Fabric = t kan'
125. Fire = agon
126. Fly = lit'at
127. God = bok
128. Give = davit
129. Hello = zdrastvuytye
130. Hole = dyra
131. Home = dom
132. Honesty = chyesny
133. Hungry = galo'dny
134. Husband = muzh
135. Write = pisat
136. Conlibiac = loaf of fish, meat or vegetable baked in pastry shell
137. Medovukha = A Russian honey-based alcoholic beverage
138. Okroshka = A type of Russian cold soup with mixed raw vegetable
139. Shchi = A type of Cabbage soup
140. Babushka = Grandmother, granny, or just old woman
141. Inteligensia = Intelligence
142. Duma = To think, or to consider
143. Chlysty = Christ- believers, Christianity
144. Bespopovtsy = Old believers
145. Dosaaf = Free will or Voluntary, Navy, Military
146. Banya = Steam bath

147. Bylina = Occurred
148. VodKa = A 40% alcoholic liquor
149. Burlak = homeless

Greek:

1. Hello = Kheh- reh-the
2. Goodbye = yah sahs
3. Yes = neh
4. Ok = ehn- dah- ksee
5. No = oh khee
6. I'd like = thah-ee theh- lah
7. How much? = Poh-soh
8. where is? = Poo ee neh
9. Please = Pah- rah-kah-loh
10. Excuse me = Pah- rah-kah-loh

11. you are welcome = pah- rah-kah- loh
12. could you speak more slowly? = hoh- ree-the- nah-mee-lah-the-pioh-ahr-ghah
13. I don't understand = thehn- kah-tah-lah-veh-noh
14. do you speak Greek? = Mee-lah- the ahn gklee- kah
15. where is the restroom? = poo-ee-neh ee too oh leh tah?
16. Help = voh-ee-thee-ah
17. I am just passing through = ohp-lohs pehr-nah-ah-poh-eh thoh
18. I have nothing to declare = Thehneh-khoh-nah-thee-loh-soh-tee-poh tah
19. Customs = the-loh-nee-oh
20. Duty-free goods = ah-foh-roh-loh-yee-tah-ee thee
21. age = seem-foh-noh
22. air conditioning = Klee- mah – teez- mohs
23. animal = zoh-oh
24. arm = kheh-ree
25. art = tekh-nee
26. baby = moh-roh
27. baggage = ah-pohs- keh- yehs
28. bakery = ah- rtoh-pee-ee-oh
29. bank = trah-peh-zah
30. blind = peh- rsee- thels
31. boot = boh-tah
32. body = soh-mah
33. bowel = ehn- deh-roh
34. boxing = bohks
35. boy = ah-ghoh-ree
36. bridge = yeh-fee-rah
37. brush = voor – tsah

38. build = ktee-zoh
39. building = ktee-ree-oh
40. burn = eh- gah-mah
41. bus stop = stah-see-leh oh foh-ree-oo
42. butcher shop = kreh-oh- poh-lee-oh
43. café = kah-feh-the-ree-ah
44. bedroom = eep-noh-thoh-mah-tee-oh
45. blood = eh-mah
46. broom = skoo-pah
47. business = bee znehs
48. call = klee-see
49. complain = pah-rah-poh-nieh-meh
50. computer = ee-poh-loh-yee-stees
51. condom = proh-fee-tah-ktee-koh
52. cancer = kahr-kee-nohs
53. court house = thee-kahs-tee-ree-oh
54. crown = koh-roh-nah
55. cup = flee-jah-nee
56. damage = zee-miah
57. dangerous = eh-pee-keen-thee-nohs
58. degrees = vohth-me
59. delicious = nohs-tee-mohs
60. dentist = oh thohn-dee-ah-trohs
61. doctor = yah-trohs
62. diving = kah-tah-thee-tee
63. direction = oh thee- yee-ah
64. door = pohr-tah

65. divorced = thee-ah- zehv-ghmeh- nohs
66. drink = poh-toh-pee-noh
67. easy = ehf- koh-lohs
68. eat = troh-oh
69. example = pah-rah-theegh-mah
70. exit = eh-ksoh-thohs
71. fabric = ee-fahs-mah
72. face = proh- sah-poh
73. fall = pehf-toh
74. fan = ah-neh-mees-tee-rahs
75. far = mahk-ree-ah
76. fat = pah-khees
77. favorite = ah-ghah-pee-meh-nohs
78. ear = ahf-tee
79. feed = tah-ee-zoh
80. finger =thakh-tee-loh
81. fire = foh-tiah
82. fire escape = eh-ksoh-thohs keen-thee-noo
83. first class = proh-tee theh-see
84. flat = eh-pee-peh- thohs
85. flood = plee-mee-rah
86. flower = loo-loo-thee
87. fly = peh- tah-eh
88. foreign = Kseh-nohs
89. free = eh-lehf-theh-rohs
90. fresh = frehs-kohs
91. friend = fee-lohs

92. from = ah-poh
93. gift = thoh-roh
94. girl = koh-ree-tsee
95. glass = poh-tee-ree
96. glove = ghahn-dee
97. gold = khree- sohs
98. go = pee-yeh-noh
99. Greece = eh-lah-Thah
100. Hair = mah-liah
101. Half = mee-sohs
102. Hand = kheh-ree
103. Hat = kah-peh-loh
104. handle = poh-meh-loh
105. hospital = noh-soh-koh-mee- oh
106. illegal = pah-rah-noh-mohs
107. illness = ahr-ohs-tee-ah
108. injection = eh-neh-see
109. injured = trahv-mah-teez-meh-nohs
110. invitation = prohs-klee-see
111. iron = see- theh roh
112. insurance = ahs-fah-lee-ah
113. jacket = sah-kah-kee
114. jar = yah-zoh
115. jaw = sah-ghoh-nee
116. knife = mah-kheh-ree
117. laugh = yeh-loh
118. library = veev-lee-oh-thee-kee

119. loose = fahr-thees
120. lotion = loh-siohn
121. loud = thee-nah-tohs
122. love = ah- ghah- poh
123. lunch = meh-see – mehr-yah-noh
124. main = kee-ree-ohs
125. map = khahr- tees
126. massage = mah-sahz
127. message = mee-nee-mah
128. metal = meh-tah-loh
129. mobile phone = kee-nee-toh
130. money = khree-mah-tah
131. must = preh-pee
132. Move = meh-tah-koh-mee-zoh
133. Mouth = stah-mah
134. Narrow = steh-nohs
135. Name = oh-noh-mah
136. Old = pah-liohs
137. old-fashioned = deh- mohn- deh
138. once = miah-foh- rah
139. paper = khar-tee
140. paint = zohgh-rah-fee-zoh
141. permit = ah-thee-ah
142. pickup = pehr-noh
143. police = ah-stee-noh-mee-ah
144. quiet = ee-see-khohs
145. ready = eh-tee-mohs

Greek

146. right = soh-stohs
147. river = poh-tah-mohs
148. snow = khioh-nee-zee
149. south = noh-tee-ohs
150. wrong = lah-thohs

Hindi:

1. Go straight = see-de-joa-o
2. cheap ticket = sas-taa-tiket
3. a man = ek/ ko- ee- aad-mee
4. I = mayng
5. You = to
6. you are = hay
7. they = vo = hayng
8. he is British- Voh-an-grez hay
9. This room is full = yeh kam raa ba rea hay
10. this hotel = yeh hotal

11. those ones = voh
12. what's that = voh kyaa hay
13. how much does this coat cost? = is kot kaa daam kyaa hay?
14. she works = voh kam kar tee hay
15. she doesn't work = voh kam no beeng kar tee
16. could you please? = me-har-baa-nee-kar ke
17. what time is it? = Ta aim kyaa hay
18. what date is today? = aaj kyaa toa-reek-hay
19. Spring = vas ant
20. Summer = gar-mee ke din
21. Autumn = pat-jar
22. Winter = sar dee
23. Week = is hafte
24. Year = issaal
25. yesterday = kal
26. which goes to = (Karachi kaun-see (ka- roa) Chee= Jaa tee hay
27. first = Peh-lee
28. next = ag-lee
29. last = aaki-ree
30. Is this seat available? = Kyaa yeh seet kaa lee hay
31. my luggage = me- raa-saa – man
32. duty-free shop = dyee tee free
33. gate = get (teen)
34. please go straight to this address = is ee ja gah to fan ran jaa i- ye
35. I feel like going to a = jaa ne kaa man ra haa hay
36. Café = kay fe
37. Party = paar- tee

39. I don't take drugs = mayng ne- shee-lee da von oag ka
40. do you have a light? = maa- chis hay
41. religion = maz-hab
42. I am not religious = me – raa- ka ee maz hab na heeng hay
43. Catholic = kay to lik
44. Christian = ee- saa-ee
45. Hindu = bin-doa
46. Muslim = musal maan
47. Sikh = sik
48. Jewish = jayn
49. Zoroastrian = paar-see
50. cultural differences = Threani- akhtela
51. I'm sorry, it is against my = maaf kee ji-ye- yeh me re ke-vi rud hay.
52. I didn't mean to do/say anything wrong = maaf kee ji ye jaan booj kar mayng nen yeh ha heeng ki yaa/ka haa
53. Shortest = cho-taa
54. Toilets = taa-I – let
55. Showers = na-haa-ne kee
56. Cold = tand
57. Hot = ba- hut- gar-mee
58. Snowing = barf par- rahee
59. Sunny = doop
60. Warm = gar-mee
61. season= kaa-mau sam
62. flood = se-laab
63. dry = soo-kaa
64. animal = joan- var

65. flower = pool
66. plant = puu-daa
67. tree = per
68. breakfast = noash-tea
69. lunch = din-kaa-kaa-naa
70. to eat = kaa- naa
71. to drink = pee- naa
72. bar = ek baar
73. restaurant = res to rent
74. bill = bil
75. menu = men-yoo
76. God = Khoda
77. what would you recommend? = aap ke kyat meng kyaa ach chaa ho gaa
78. breads = ro tee naan
79. soup = soups
80. salt = na mak
81. vinegar = sirkaa
82. spicy = ba- hut tee kaa
83. oily = ba hut tel
84. I'd like it = mu- je chaa hi ye
85. Boiled = ab- laa
86. Fried = ta-laa
87. Medium = kam-pa kaa
88. Steamed = baapse
89. well done = ach chee ta rah pa kaa
90. fire! = Aaq
91. hot water = garm-paa-nee

92. water = paa – nee
93. a bottle of = Wine= sha raab kee bo-tal
94. excuse me = su – ni – ye
95. beef = gosht
96. same again, please = va – hee-pitse dee ji ye
97. less = kam
98. what's the local specialty? = kaas lo kal cheet kyaa hay
99. I'd like = mu- je… chaa- hi- ye
100. dairy products = ba-nee- chee-zong
101. garlic = lah- sun
102. fish = mach-lee
103. eggs = an-de
104. onion = pyeaz
105. thief = chor
106. go away! = Joa- o
107. watch out = ka- bar- daar
108. it's an emergency = I – mar- jen- see- hay
109. wallet = ba-tu-aa
110. I didn't do It = mayng ne na heeng ki you
111. I 'm sick= mayng bee maar hoong
112. heart attack = dil kaa dour aa
113. I feel dizzy = chak- kar-aa- ra – baa hay-
114. I have = mu- je. Hay
115. Massage = malish
116. Drug = ba- nee-da- vaa
117. Salts = salts
118. I have a cavity = ek daant meng ched hay

Hindi

119. a board = savaar
120. gay = kosh
121. go = jaa-naa
122. good = ach- chaa
123. half = aa- daa
124. hire = ki raa ye par le naa
125. job = nouk-ree
126. marry = shad- dee= kar – naa
127. name = naam
128. now = ab
129. old = pu-raa- naa
130. open = kulaa
131. soon = jal- dee= early= fast
132. souvenir = ni- shaa- nee
133. spring = ba-haar
134. stop = lehr- naa
135. T.V. = lee vee
136. Vacant = kaa-lee
137. Warm = garm
138. Write = likh-naa
139. Dark = daam
140. Toothache = dant meng dard
141. Knife = chaa koo
142. dirty = gan-daa
143. expensive = shob-doh
144. small = choh-toh
145. shoes = ju-ta
146. I'll think about it = chin-ta – koh- re – nay

147. how much is it? = e ta k otoh
148. what's that? = oh-ta ki
149. what's your phone number? = aap-nar fohn nom bohr ki
150. I 'd like to see = aa- mi dek – te chai

Southwest Black Bean Burgers

Prep: 20 minutes

Cook: 31 minutes

Level: Immmediate

Yield: 6 servings

You don't have to be a vegetarian to enjoy this flavorful burger made with black beans, salsa and chopped fresh cilantro.

Ingredients

- 1/4 cup dry bread crumbs
- 3 Tbsp. KRAFT Real Mayo Mayonnaise
- 1 tsp. ground cumin
- 1/4 tsp. ground red pepper (cayenne)
- 2 cans (15 oz. each) black beans, rinsed, divided
- 2 stalks celery, finely chopped
- 1/4 cup chopped fresh cilantro
- 6 KRAFT Singles
- 6 whole-wheat hamburger buns
- 6 lettuce leaves
- 1/3 cup TACO BELL® Thick & Chunky Salsa
- 1/3 cup BREAKSTONE'S or KNUDSEN Sour Cream

Preparation Directions

1- Use pulsing action to process bread crumbs, mayo, seasonings and half the beans in food processor until well blended. Transfer to large bowl; mix in celery, cilantro, and remaining beans. Shape into 6 (1/2-inch-thick) patties.

2- Cook in skillet sprayed with cooking spray on medium-high heat 5 min. on each side or until done (160°F). Top with Singles; cook 1 min. or until melted.

3- Fill buns with lettuce, cheeseburgers, salsa, and sour cream.

Brazilian (Portuguese):

1. A lot = Mutio
2. Accident = acidente
3. achieve, to = conse guir
4. Action = acao
5. Actress = atriz
6. Address = endereco
7. Answer = the phone, = a tender telephone
8. Any = qualquer
9. Arrest = prender
10. Art = arte
11. Artist = artista

12. at the same time = mesmo tempo
13. attack = ataque
14. aunt = tie
15. bad = ruim
16. bag = bolsa
17. baggage = bagagem
18. bald = careca
19. bath = banho
20. beautiful = lindo, linda
21. beef = camedeboi
22. beer = cerveja
23. blind = cego
24. blond = louro, loura
25. blue = azul
26. book = livro
27. both = ambos, ambas
28. bread = pao
29. bride = noira
30. couple = casal
31. cousin(f) = prima
32. cousin(m) = primo
33. cultural = cultura
34. crime = crime
35. dentist = exigir
36. dial tone = sinal
37. dish = prato
38. divided = dividido

39. drunk = bebado
40. easy = facil
41. egg = ovo
42. embassy = embaixada
43. engineer = engenheiro
44. enjoy to = curtir
45. error = mistake= arro
46. escape = fuga
47. Excellent = excelente
48. Excited = animado
49. Sorry = comlicenca
50. exist to = haver
51. facing, in front of = defronte de
52. fast = rapido
53. factory worker = operario (m) operaria(f)
54. famous = Famoso, = famosa
55. Father = pai
56. Frog = sapo
57. Garage = garage
58. get to = conseguir
59. give to = dar
60. go out = (leave to) = sair
61. go to bed = deitar- se
62. God = deus
63. Good = boa-bom
64. good luck = boa sorte
65. grammar = gramatica

66. handset = gancho
67. hangover = ressaca
68. happy = contente- feliz
69. he = ele
70. heart = coracao
71. hello = alo
72. help = Socorro
73. her = dela
74. himself = si
75. hot = calor
76. hour = hora
77. house = casa
78. how many? = quantos- or quantas
79. how much? = quanto- quanta
80. hug = abraco
81. humor = humor
82. hunt = caca
83. husband = marrido
84. idea = ideia
85. identical = identico
86. illegal = illegal
87. insistence = insistencia
88. instructor = instructor
89. intelligent = inteligente
90. inventor = inventor
91. Iranian = iraniano
92. Iraq = Iraque

93. Israel = Israel
94. Judge = juiz= juiza
95. Key = chave
96. King = Rei
97. Kiss = beijo
98. lesson= licao
99. liberty= Liberdade
100. liqueur= licor
101. lose to= perder
102. love= amar
103. may= poder
104. melon= melao
105. merry chrismas= Feliz natal
106. message= recado
107. milk = leite
108. mirror = espelho
109. miserable= miseravel
110. miss to = fezer falta
111. moment= momento
112. paid= pago
113. pencil= lapis
114. perfume= perfume
115. people= gente
116. personal= infinitive
117. paper= papel
118. park= parquet
119. party= festa

120. pass, to= passer
121. pen= caneta
122. pay, to = pagar
123. peach= pessego
124. pediatrician= pediatra
125. persistent= persistente
126. physical= fisico
127. pig's ear= orelha de porco
128. pilot= piloto
129. place= lugar
130. planet= planeta
131. play= jogar
132. pleasure= prazer
133. pity= do'
134. raw= cru- crua
135. reflect to= reflector
136. remembrance= lembranca
137. reptile= reptile
138. rice= arroz
139. rifle= fuzil
140. said= ditto
141. salt= sal
142. same= mesmo
143. school= escola
144. she= ela
145. sick = doente
146. single = solteiro

Potuguese

147. sister = irma'
148. sleep to = dormer
149. talent = talent
150. tree = arvore

Mushroom and Epazote Tacos

Prep: 10 minutes

Cook: 5 minutes

Level: Immmediate

Yield: 6 servings

Ingredients

- Guerrero® Yellow Corn Tortillas - 12
- Vegetable oil - 4 Tablespoons
- Button mushrooms - 2 Cups, sliced
- Poblano peppers - 2, roasted, peeled, and cut into strips
- White onion - 1, cut into strips
- Epazote - 2 Tablespoons, washed and chopped
- Sour cream - ½ Cup
- Cacique® queso fresco - ¼ Cup
- Sea salt
- Pepper

Preparation Directions

1- In a medium-size skillet, heat the oil over high heat and add the onions; cook until translucent, add the mushrooms and poblano peppers. Cover and let it cook for 3-4 minutes.

2- Add the epazote and season with salt and pepper. Add the sour cream and mix in. Remove from the heat and set aside.

3- Warm tortillas on a hot comal, fill with them with the creamy mushrooms, top with queso fresco and enjoy.

Turkish:

1. Gu'zel = beautiful
2. gu'zellik = beauty
3. Mutlu = happy
4. Mutluluk = happiness
5. Iyi = good
6. Iyilik = goodness
7. Zor = difficult
8. Zorluk = difficulty
9. arkadasimin mutluugu mu kendi mutulugumdan daha o'nemlidir? = is my girlfriend's happiness more important than my own happiness?
10. gu'zelligine = its beauty (gu'zel-lig-i-n-e)

11. su manzaranin gu'zelligne bakin! = regard the beauty of this view!
12. Zorluklarimiz = our difficulties
13. tabi bu zorluklarimiz oldu oma hicbir zaman bu zorluklarimizdan yilmadik! = we are subject to difficulties, but we have never been afraid of our difficulties!
14. Baba = father
15. Babacik = daddy
16. Kedi = cat
17. Kediciki = pussy cat
18. ko'pek = dog
19. ko'pecik = puppy
20. otobu's hat ve gu'zergahlari kitapcigi = auto bus line and routes booklet
21. hosgeldin arkadascigim! = welcome my dear friend!
22. ku'cu'k = small
23. ku'cu'cu'k = little
24. ufak = small ufacik = tiny, minute
25. minik = small and nice
26. minicik = wee, tiny
27. az = less
28. azicik = little less
29. as in birazicik = just a little
30. bir = one
31. biricik = unique
32. dar = narrow
33. daracik = narrowish
34. -im = my
35. baba cigim = my daddy
36. ko'pecigim! = my little puppy

37. genc = young
38. genclik = youth
39. yasli = old
40. yaslilik = the aged
41. insan = person
42. insanlik = humam-kind
43. kisi = person/individual
44. kisilik = personality/ identity
45. bakan = minister
46. bakanlik = ministry
47. bakanligi = ministry of justice
48. balik = fish
49. balikci = fisherman
50. balikcilik = fishing club, group, association
51. tuz = salt
52. tuzluk = salt cellar
53. biber = papper
54. biberlik = pepper shaker
55. go'z = eye
56. go'zlu'k = spectacles
57. kira = hire
58. kiralik = for hire
59. yagmur = rain
60. yagmurluk = rain coat
61. bakanlik binasi = ministry building
62. camasir = laundry
63. camasirlik = laundry room

64. bahce = rock garden
65. orman = forest
66. ormanlikalan = forested area
67. ormanda cok yabani hayvan varmis = it seems there are many wild animals in that forest.
68. elmalik = apple orchard
69. elma = apple
70. sebzelik = vegetable garden
71. sebze = vegetable
72. ciceklik = flower garden
73. cicek = flower
74. Kitaplik = bookcase
75. Kitab = book
76. on yumurta = ten eggs
77. sabir = patience
78. on yumurtalik bir kutu istiyorum. = I want ten eggs
79. iki kisilik cadir var mi? = is there a tent of two people? Double tent."
80. evet var. kac gu'nlu'k? = yes, there is how many days?
81. sabirsiz = impatient
82. dikkat = care
83. dikkatsiz = careless
84. kapinin zili = the door bell (kapi-nin- zil-i)
85. isik diregi= lamp post
86. ali nin elma agaci= Ali's apple tree.
87. deniz suyu = the sea water
88. Kadin dektoru = lady doctor.
89. otobu's duragi= bus stop

90. polis orabasi = police car
91. meyve suyu = fruit juice
92. et suyu = gravy
93. elma suyu = apple juice
94. pinar suyu = spring water
95. cep telefonlari = mobile phone
96. tahta kapi = wooden door
97. camasir makineleri = washing machines
98. demir ko'pru' = iron bridge
99. odada = in the room
100. nakit = cash
101. Yatakta = on the bed
102. Masada = from the table
103. Cevaptan = from the answer
104. c, ay pahali = tea is expensive
105. banka = bank
106. cay soguk = the tea is cold
107. og'ul = from the son
108. araba caddede = the car is in the road
109. adam kapiyi = the man closed the door
110. Fikir = idea
111. Kutu = box
112. Evim = my house
113. Evimi = my house
114. adam kilidimi = the man locked
115. kilid – im- i. = my lock
116. agizda = in the mouth

Turkish

117. keyif = joy
118. beyinden = from the brain
119. isimim = my name
120. kayiptan = from the loss

Ayran with Mint or Yogurt drink

Prep: 2 minutes

Immmediate

Cook: 3 minutes

Level:

Yield: 1 serving

This is very similar to plain Ayran. However, mint is added to provide a refreshing taste during hot summers of Anatolia.

Turkish

Ingredients:

- 1-pint plain yogurt (the thicker the better)
- Several ices cube
- A generous pinch of salt
- A little chopped fresh mint
- 1-pint water

Preparation Directions

1. Add yogurt and water to a blender.
2. Add ice cubes and salt. Add a bit of fresh mint, optional.
3. Blend until well mixed.
4. Serve.

References:

New Testament Greek

Japanese in plain English

Beginner's Russian

Book bridges for ESL students

Beginner's French dictionary

Barron's E_Z Spanish

Berlitz Greek phrase book

Chinese

English for coming Americans

Essential Arabic: speak Arabic

Easy Russian phrase book

English through the ages

Italian in 10 minutes

Instant German

Learn French

Spanish the easy way

Side by side Italian & English grammar

Hindi Urdu & Bengali

Teaching English as a second language

Teach yourself Hindi dictionary

The everything Brazilian Portuguese Phrase.

Printed by Libri Plureos GmbH in Hamburg, Germany